If you were me and lived in...
MEXICO...

A Child's Introduction to Cultures Around the World

Carole P. Roman

To my four wonders of the world-
Sharon, Michael, Jennifer and Eric

Copyright © 2013 Carole P. Roman

All rights reserved.

ISBN: 1480209627

ISBN 13: 9781480209626

Library of Congress Control Number: 2012921018

CreateSpace Independent Publishing Platform, North Charleston, SC

MEXICO CITY

MEXICO

If you were me and lived in Mexico, your home would be somewhere here, in the southern part of North America.

2

You might live near the capital city. It is called Mexico City and is very old. There are many historic buildings like the Palacio de Bellas Artes, which is the Palace of Fine Arts.

4

When you talk to your Mommy you would call her Mamá, and when you speak with your Daddy, you would call him Papá.

If you asked your parents for money, they might give you a peso.

10

If you had a visitor you would take them to Chichen Itza. It is a Mayan Temple shaped like a pyramid and is very old. There are 365 steps on it, one for each day of the year.

12

Afterward, you would go for something tasty to eat. Your favorite could be a tamale. It is a mixture of meat and corn dough wrapped in corn husks. Sometimes it is spicy or sometimes it can be sweet and made with pineapples. But it is always delicious.

 14

If you watch a sport, it would probably be fútbol. It is a very popular sport and also known as soccer.

If you chose to play with a doll, you would call her la muñeca.

16

You would love to celebrate a holiday called Descubrimiento de América. It is a day to honor the discovery of America by Christopher Columbus in 1492. Do you have a special day like that too?

18

You would learn all about that
in a place called la escuela.
Can you guess what that is?

So now you see, if you were me, how life in Mexico could really be.

22

Pronunciation

Palacio de Bellas Artes (Pa-LA-cio day bay-yas-Ar-tes)

Alejandro (A-le-HAN-dro)

Santiago (San-Tia-go)

Nicolás (Ni-co_LAS)

Camila (ca-Mil-la)

Isabella (Is-a-bel-la)

Sophía (So-Fee-a)

Mamá (ma-Ma)

Papá (pa-Pa)

Peso (Pe-so)

Chichen Itza (che-Chin-it-sa)

Fútbol (FT-bol)

Tamale (Ta-Mal-ayes)

Muñeca (mu-NIE-ca)

Descubrimiento (des-cu-bri-Mein-to)

Escuela (es-Kwe-la)